JACK AND THE BEANSTALK

A Basic Pantomime

by

P. H. ADAMS

and

CONRAD CARTER

LONDON

NEW YORK TORONTO SYDNEY HOLLYWOOD

ISBN 0 573 06428 8

PREFACE.

Of all our national forms of entertainment, the Pantomime is perhaps the most traditional and shows least signs of waning popularity. The average " run " of the professional pantomime is certainly as long as ever, and for many years it has been a source of considerable enjoyment and profit among amateur societies.

It is for this latter field of activity that this series of " BASIC PANTOMIME " has been specially designed, both as regards the " scripts," the settings, and the general production problems which face every company in work of this type.

Apart from the time-honoured stories on which all our pantomimes are (and rightly) based, much of their success depends on topicality, local and current humour, and by no means least upon the songs and choruses of the time—even of the year.

With this in view, these " basic " pantomimes have been prepared, not as the final, unalterable show, but as *bases* upon which may be built the ultimate product according to the desires, and the resources, of the individual company.

The scripts follow, in each case, the traditional stories very strictly. Any major departure would be resented by the youngest—and the oldest !—members of the audience. The dialogue is in modern prose, and prepared so that " cuts," additions, and the introduction of " local " or " topical " references may be effected with a minimum of difficulty.

Simplicity has been the prior aim also with regard to the settings, which are dealt with in detail in the "Production Notes" for each of the scripts. These contain suggestions for yet further simplification where the exigencies of the theatre are exceptionally limited, as well as indications of elaboration for those who are more fortunately placed.

Equal consideration has been given to the matter of Musical Numbers, Dances, etc. Those indicated represent what may be regarded as a reasonable minimum ; in fact, where resources are available, one or two extra numbers might be added with advantage. But the basic form which the pantomimes take render these additions quite easy to effect.

On the other hand, it will be found that, if desired, the pantomimes may be produced without alteration in any department despite the title of "BASIC" which has, for the foregoing reasons, been conferred upon them.

JACK AND THE BEANSTALK

CHARACTERS:

JACK.
WIDOW TWANKEY (his mother).
MR. EGG (the bailiff).
MR. CHIPS (his assistant).
ODOROUS EGG (the bailiff's sister).
JILL (the giant's servant maid).
GIANT SNUFFLEGOBBLER.
AN OLD WOMAN (a fairy).
CLARIBELLE (the cow).

Chorous of School Children, Villagers, Herald, Pages, etc.
Ballet of Fairies.

ACT I.

SCENE 1. *A Cottage Garden.*
SCENE 2. *The Road to Market.*
SCENE 3. }
SCENE 4. } *The same as Scene 1.*

ACT II.

SCENE 1. *The Road to the Giant's Castle.*
SCENE 2. *The Giant's Kitchen.*
SCENE 3. *The Road from the Castle.*
SCENE 4. *The Cottage Garden.* (As Act I, Sc. 1.).

MUSICAL NUMBERS.

ACT I.

SCENE 1.

No. 1.	OPENING CHORUS ...	(*School Children*)
2.	SONG	(WIDOW TWANKEY)

SCENE 2.

No. 3.	CHORUS	(*Villagers*)
4.	SONG (*with Dance*)	(JACK, *and the Cow*)
5.	SONG	(CHIPS)

SCENE 3.

No. 6.	DANCE	(*The* FAIRIES)

ACT II.

SCENE 1 (*Front of tabs, after scene*)

No. 7.	PATTER SONG ...	(WIDOW TWANKEY)

SCENE 2.

No. 8.	SONG	(JILL)
9.	DUET	(JACK *and* JILL)
10.	DUET	(ODOROUS *and* EGG)
(*Front of tabs, after scene*)		
11.	SONG (*with refrain and dance*) ...	(CHORUS)

SCENE 3.

No. 12	DUET	(JACK *and* JILL)
13	SONG	(CHIPS)
(*Front of tabs, after scene*)		
14.	DANCE (*Fairies*) *or* SPECIALITY NUMBER	(*Any Character*)

SCENE 4.

No. 15.	TRIO (*Ref. and Dance*)	(WIDOW, EGG *and* CHIPS)
16.	FINALE	(FULL COMPANY)

PRODUCTION NOTES.

Settings.

On referring to the ground plans it will be seen that care has been taken to design the settings for the quickest and easiest possible scene changes. Cloths, wings, and ground rows form the major part of the material involved, with the minimum use of flats for interior scenes.

A " sky-cloth " is set at the extreme back of the stage and this remains, and is employed, throughout. The simplest of wing-pieces, or cut-outs together with lighting changes will produce most successful variations of scene. Other cloths are lowered at varying stage depths, and some of these may also be plain sky-cloths if used in conjunction with the above " pieces."

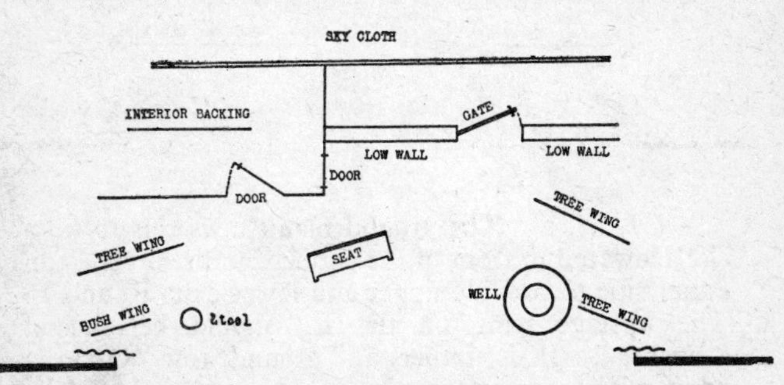

Act I, Sc. I. Back stage, R. of the centre, is the cottage, the only piece of " solid " scenery needed, and this, together with the sky-cloth, can remain untouched throughout the show, provided a reasonable stage depth is still left to work upon. A low brick wall runs from the left wall of the cottage to disappear behind a masking wing on the prompt side. There should be a gate slightly on the L. side of C.

The one important point about the cottage is the growth of the beanstalk. This, in the first instance, appears and grows for a few feet upstage and slightly to the L. of the left wall, at the close of Scene 3. When the lights fade in on Scene 4, the beanstalk is fully grown, and extends to above the roof of the cottage. As will be seen under the heading of "Effects," it will be necessary to have a cut in the left wall, covered during the first scene by a canvas panel to match the rest of the wall. The garden seat should have a solid back, to mask the growing beanstalk until it appears above the level of the seat. The well is an easily constructed prop, made of wood and three-ply—if possible strong enough to sit upon—and having a winding handle, and a rope which coils in the central depression. The remainder of the setting consists of simple "tree wings."

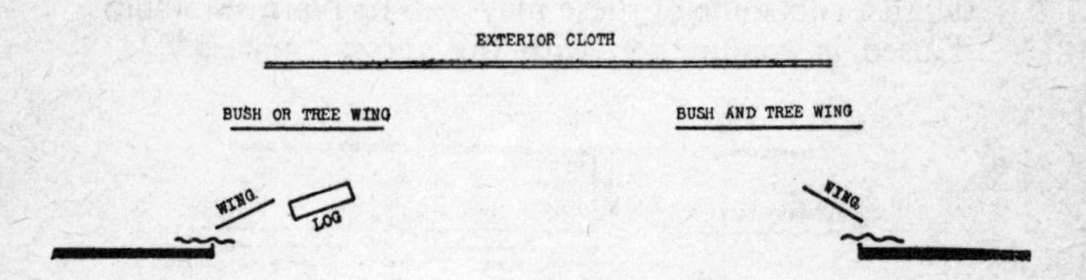

Act I, Sc. 2. The ground plan shows this to be a cloth lowered in front of the cottage, and two wings on either side to provide upper and lower exits R. and L. The upstage wing on the L., should be one of "bushes." It is rather a "ground row" than a wing. The downstage wing on either side should be high, and represent trees, to mask in the extremities of the cloth, which may be a sky-cloth, or a painted exterior.

To simplify, it may be possible on some stages to employ the sky-cloth of Scene 1, and mask the cottage with a more extensive tree wing. In these circumstances, the low brick wall must be struck for Scene 2.

Act I, Scenes 3 *and* 4. These are the same as for Scene 1, and need no comment other than the suggestions under " Effects."

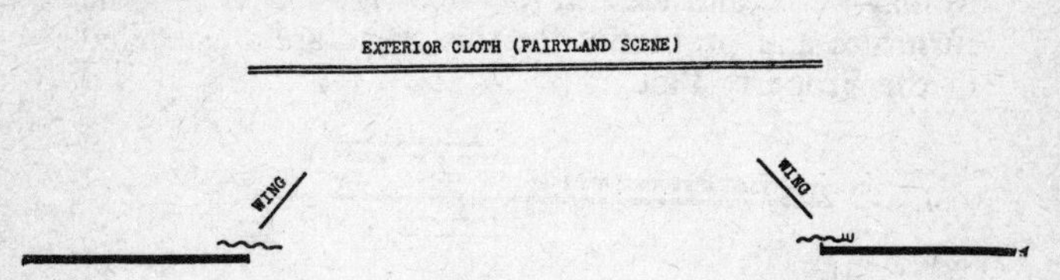

Act II, Scene 1. This is " The Road to the Giant's Castle " and, to be most effective, requires a cloth of a rather special type, though not difficult to obtain. The ground plan shows it as a simple cloth, and wings, but it is suggested that a " cut cloth " should be used, and employed also for Scene 3 (The " Road *from* the Castle.") If, however, a simple cloth is used, it can be a sky-cloth with wings suggestive of something mysterious and fairylike rather than " real world." For the alternative, see *Scene* 3.

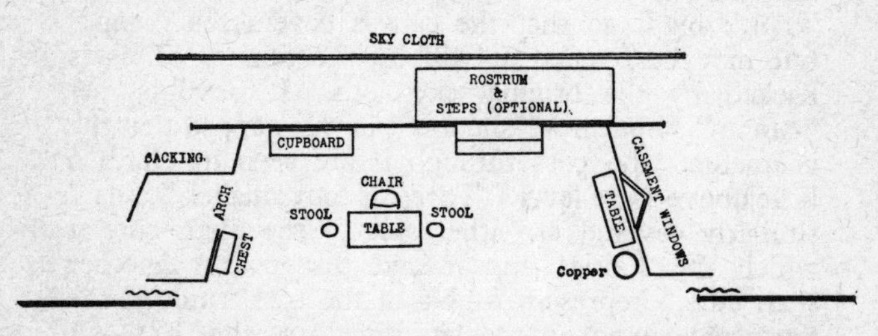

Act II, Scene 2. (*The Giant's Kitchen.*) Strictly speaking, as this is an interior, a set composed of flats should be employed. For facility in change, however, the ground plan shows an " interior cut cloth " to form the back wall, the cut being a doorway (no door) somewhat L. of C. Then, side flats are run in on each side, that on the right having a similar, but smaller doorway, while that on the left has a casement window which can be opened, and through which an entrance can be made. The Act I sky-cloth provides the backing to the main doorway. A rostrum and step down here would be effective, and if resorted to may be set and used in the "cottage scenes." The furniture and properties for this scene are all detailed in the Property Plot.

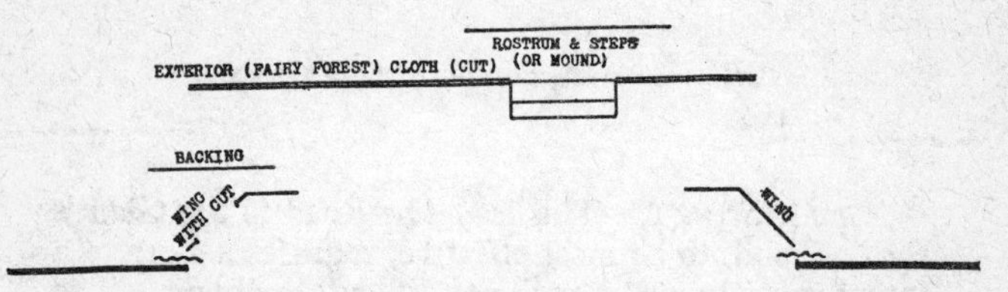

Act II, Scene 3. ("*The Road* from *the Castle.*") This scene necessitates the "cut-cloth" mentioned under "Scene 1," for which it can also be used. It should be painted a pale misty grey-green, or grey-blue with no definite features except perhaps at the sides, and these merely vague outlines of strange, fairy-land trees. At C., or slightly to L. of C., a large "cut," made so that the canvas covers the "gap" but may be opened at will by the fairies. This is backed by the original sky-cloth. If possible, set "stone" steps, or a "mound" in this gap, so that the characters who pass through it are seen to climb a little above stage level. Three or four smaller "cuts" similarly covered on either side of the main cut, at which the Fairies appear and disappear. Another such cut to represent a hole in the tree trunk in the downstage wing on the left, for JACK and JILL. A similar cut may be made in the tree down R., for another Fairy but this is not essential. The colour, and the plainness of the back cloth is important in order that the moving shadows of house may be cast on it by the flicker wheel in the "run across" business.

Act II, Scene 4. This is the same as for Act I, and requires no further comment.

EFFECTS.

In " Jack and the Beanstalk " there are a minimum of " magical " effects. The lighting cues assist the disappearance of fairies, and so on.

The most important effect is that of the " beanstalk." For Scene 3, in Act I, it is merely seen to grow before the eyes of the audience to a height of a few feet. The beanstalk on this occasion is made of hessian or canvas, with such tendrils and side-shoots as make it appear convincing. It is set to the left of the left corner of the cottage, masked by the garden seat, and attached to a strong thin wire which runs up to a hidden pulley, and so drawn up slowly from off stage.

In Scene 4, the beanstalk is fully grown, and it is possible to climb up it. It should now be of greater girth, have more mature tendrils, and is made of narrow strips of green canvas sewn to a net background. It is attached to, and hides, a ladder, or a pair of household steps. If the latter, these are set in the " gap " in the left wall of the cottage (the opening masked so far as possible) and it only remains to ensure that characters climbing up " disappear " effectively. The simplest means for this is as follows:

A tree border is hung over the roof of the cottage, extending to within two or three feet of the left edge of the roof. From the left edge of this border there is an extension of theatrical gauze which will be indistinguishable to the audience during the earlier scenes. This gauze should have an irregularly curved edge towards the left. When the lights fade-in on Scene 4, the flood on the sky-cloth is dimmed down *and confined solely to the prompt side half, and not reaching quite to the centre.* At the same time, the stage lighting from the side of the spectator, *i.e.*, floats and battens *below* the cottage, render any character climbing the beanstalk and reaching eventually *behind* the gauze, quite invisible. There must be, of course, a hidden platform above the roof on to which the characters pass and thence off stage. By a nice adjustment of lighting the characters are not sharply cut off, but disappear mistily. It must be remembered that at this point there is much excitement going on below, on the stage, upon which the attention of the audience will be chiefly focused, and this will assist the illusion. A similar adjustment of lighting must be made for the final scene when the characters descend.

THE ECHO can be spoken by a character through a megaphone, or an electrical amplifier. The effect to be aimed at is " mystery " rather than excessive loudness.

THUNDER and LIGHTNING FLASHES require respectively a suspended sheet of iron and magnesium flash-lights, or any electrical flash mechanism the regulations permit for safety.

The HEN can be made (with golden egg inserted and released at will) or hired from a firm of conjurer's apparatus.

CLARIBELLE the Cow will be played by two persons, for whom the costume may be hired.

A DUMMY of the GIANT for Act II, Scene 4, and thrown from the roof is more convincing than only the hat and money bags, etc. The dummy should be so thrown that it reaches the stage *above* the garden wall and so hidden thereby.

COSTUMES.

These are more or less traditional and can be hired. Care should be taken with regard to those for the Fairies who dance and act almost entirely in coloured spot lights. Green should be avoided as No. 7 pink spots will spoil their effect. Pink dresses are not improved by blue lighting, unless the latter are No. 16, 17, or 18 blue. White and very pale blue costumes are quite safe for lighting effects.

THE SCRIPT.

As stated in the preface, the script may be played without alteration if desired. It is complete in itself.

At the same time, a producer may have at his disposal some very individual comedians who require the material revised to suit their particular " line." Again, topical and local references always go down well if " put over " skilfully and these must of necessity be left to each producer. Some openings for these are indicated and there are many others in the script of which advantage may be taken.

There are sixteen musical numbers, including those which are done " in front of tabs " or a downstage cloth lowered for the purpose, to occupy the time involved in scene changes.

All the principal characters, except the Old Woman and the Giant, have at least one number, but the insertion of additional musical items will not be found a matter of any serious difficulty ; but such additions should be confined to points at which the dialogue is not dealing with the *story* of the play.

JACK AND THE BEANSTALK

ACT I.

SCENE I.

SCENE.—*The garden of Widow Twankey's cottage, showing the cottage exterior.* (*See Ground Plan.*)

Cottage set up R.C. Along the back, a low wall with a gate. Trees either side, below cottage, and wall. A garden seat at C. A well, and a bucket down L.

(*As the* CURTAIN RISES, *schoolchildren dance along above the wall from P.S., enter the garden, and dance, singing a chorus.*)

No. 1 *Chorus* ... (SCHOOLCHILDREN)

(*Enter* WIDOW TWANKEY *from cottage, with a basket of washing.*)

WIDOW. Get away with you, you brats ! How dare you run into my garden and trample on everything . . .

CHILDREN (*dancing round her*).—Old Widow Twankey ! Old Widow Twankey ! (*ad lib.*)

(WIDOW *puts basket down at R.C.*)

WIDOW. I'll Widow Twankey you if I catch one of you by the scruff of the neck ! And where's that good-for-nothing boy of mine, young Jack, eh ?

CHILDREN. Fishing for tiddlers ! Keeping away from his muvver ! Chasing the girls ! Yah !

WIDOW. Then be off with you, and send him back to me—go on, now . . .

(*Seizes a broom and advancing, drives them off through the gate. They shout derisively as before.*)

Go on ! Go on ! (*Bus. ad lib.*)

(*The children go into repeat of chorus and dance off P.S. the* WIDOW *shouting after them.*)

Go on ! Fetch him back ! He's as bad as the rest of you ! No good to yourselves nor no one else ! I'll tell your mothers of you—don't let me see one of your dirty faces round here again . . .

(*Exeunt* CHILDREN.)

(WIDOW *comes downstage.*)

That Jack ! The good-for-nothing scamp ! Idling his time away chasing the girls while he's supposed to be looking for a job. Just like his old man. Always too busy playing to do any work and me slaving my fingers to the bone to keep us in food and shelter. And all he leaves me when he dies is a mortgaged farm, a pile of debts and a son every bit as work-shy as he was. What a son ! Been on the dole since he left school and now they've put him on the permanent staff. Yes ! Some people take to him and although I say it you couldn't find a more attractive boy for miles around. And the way the girls get after him ! You'd think that they had never seen a man before. If only he could get hold of a rich and beautiful one—but you can't have both together. Look at me ! I'm as poor as a church mouse but—I mean ter say ! You can't have riches and beauty, and Jack won't have anything but the best lookers. Oh well ! It's no good, I shall have to get after a nice rich old gent myself. (*Giggles.*) Fancy me on the warpath at my time of life. But there, I've still got my looks and I haven't forgotten my drill. Yes—(*enthusiastically*)—I'll pay off the mortgage yet. Dear me, I'm quite excited about it.

No. 2. *Song* ... ... (WIDOW TWANKEY)

(*After number.*)

Oh dear, I'm getting too excited ! I'm all of a floo-flah ! If only I had someone to practice on . . . (*Up to gate*) . . . anyone coming ? (*Looks off P.S.*) Oh YES ! (*Disappointed*) . . . Oh, it's only Mr. Egg, the rent collector . . . worse still, he's got Mr. Chips with him—they never go down very well together ! I like a rasher, meself ! (*Comes down*) Never mind Mr. Egg will do for an exercise ! I'm pretty fresh, if he isn't ! Right-ho ! Ready for me homework !

(*She preens herself, etc., and faces across stage with a fixed smile as* EGG *and* CHIPS *enter outside fence.*)
(*Archly*) Good morning, Mr. Egg. Good morning to you, Mr. Chips. Do come in. A beautiful day, is not it ?
(*They enter gate.* EGG *is already secretly attracted to the widow and is impressed but* CHIPS *regards her disapprovingly.*)

EGG. Yes, oh yes, that is n— no . . . well, I'm not very sure.

CHIPS (*aside*). It won't be so beautiful for you in a minute.

WIDOW. I trust I see you both well ?

CHIPS (*aside*). She has not brought her specs with her !

EGG. Oh er—yes—quite—er—er—thank you.

WIDOW. I suppose you are out on business. (*Sidling up to them.*)

EGG. Yes.

WIDOW. How I envy you men. Always on the go ! Always on the go !

EGG. I—er—well—— (*Dithering bus.*)

EGG. / CHIPS } (*Together*) (*aside*). Yes, and you'll be on the go pretty soon!

WIDOW. And where are you off to this morning, Mr. Bailiff ? I'm sure you have no unpleasant duties to perform on such a lovely day.

EGG. Well—I—er—that is—we——

WIDOW (*aside*). How he stutters. I've got him cold already. (*Giggles.*) I'm as good as ever. (*To* EGG)—Oh come, Mr. Egg, I can keep a secret, especially one of yours. You're not afraid to tell me, are you ?

EGG. Why—no—of course not, but——

CHIPS. Go on, guv'nor, spit it out.

WIDOW (*freezingly*). Don't be vulgar ! (*To* EGG)—Dear Mr. Egg, I do admire your loyalty to your duty. But this once, for me, couldn't you let—er—— (*Giggles*)—couldn't you forget your duty ? Now, tell me, who is to be turned out to-day ?

EGG. Really—I—I don't like to tell you.

WIDOW (*aside*). He's weakening—Yes, he's weakening.

CHIPS. Go on, guv. Cough it up.

WIDOW. Don't be common ! (*To* EGG)—I know that we shouldn't encourage gossip and I know that you wouldn't tell anyone your business, would you ?

EGG. Er—no !

WIDOW. There ! I knew ! Dear Mr. Egg. I do admire your honesty but to show that you're not indifferent to me, tell me where you are off to to-day, won't you ?

EGG (*under pressure*). I—I'm afraid I must.

CHIPS. An' about time, too. Now for it !

WIDOW. (*aside*). Really—it was TOO easy ! (*To* EGG)—Then, dear Mr. Egg, who is the unfortunate one to-day ?

EGG. Well—it's——

WIDOW. Go on. (*Nudges him in the ribs.*)

CHIPS. Go on. (*Rubbing his palms together.*)

EGG. It's—it's——

WIDOW. Yes ?

CHIPS. Go on, Guv. Get it off your chest.

WIDOW. Don't be vulgar. (*To* EGG)—Yes, who is it ?

EGG. It's—its——

CHIPS (*in despair at* EGG *saying the word*). It's YOU !

(*The* WIDOW *is paying all attention to* EGG *and at first does not notice* CHIP'S *words, then she registers incredulity as though* CHIPS *is joking.*)

WIDOW. Don't be ridiculous. This is not a joking matter.

CHIPS. You'll soon find that out.

WIDOW. Dear Mr. Egg, please go on.

EGG. He's—he's right. I'm sorry it *is* you. I had orders to come along this morning.

WIDOW. Me ? ME ? Oh—oh—oo—h ! (*Faints.*)

(CHIPS *catches the widow and with difficulty supports her.*)

EGG (*in panic*). Lay her on her seat.

CHIPS (*breathless*). Where else d'you expect she'd lie ? (*Draws her round stage looking for seat.*)

EGG. What can we do ? What can we do ?

CHIPS. Get some burnt feathers and let her smell them.

EGG. Where ? Where ?

CHIPS. In the house. Have a look there.

(*Exit* EGG *into house while* CHIPS *continues to struggle in holding up* WIDOW. EGG *returns with a feather brush*).

CHIPS. They're no good, Guv.

EGG. No good ? But they're feathers.

CHIPS. They're not burnt feathers. It says burnt feathers in the book.

EGG. Oh—what else can we do ?

CHIPS. Water—cold water !

(EGG *gets water from well down L., and returns.*) Splash it on her face.

EGG. Yes—yes.

(*He splashes the water, but it mostly goes on* CHIPS.)

CHIPS. Oy ! Give it to me !

(*He grabs the bucket insecurely with one hand, supporting the* WIDOW *with the other. The bucket is slipping and so is* WIDOW. *Business. He eventually grabs the bucket with both hands. The* WIDOW *falls bringing* EGG *with her.* EGG *clutches* CHIPS *who also falls upsetting water over all.*)

WIDOW (*screaming*). Murder ! Police ! I'm drowning, suffocating ! I'm being murdered.

EGG. It's all right, Mum. We've got you. I'll look after you. I'll protect you. (*Holds her tenderly in his arms.*)

CHIPS. Blimey !

WIDOW. (*Screams.*) Robbers ! Thieves !

(*Pushes* EGG *away and moans, cries and rocks to and fro. They assist her to rise and get tangled with the bucket, etc. Eventually, she is placed on garden seat* EGG *trying to placate her and* CHIPS *wringing out clothes.*)

EGG (*haltingly*). I'll do anything I can to help you, Mum, but—I'm a very poor man.

WIDOW (*snivelling*). Robber ! Beast ! Oppressor of the widow, scourge of the homeless . . .

EGG (*distressed*). Oh, mum, please . . . I'm only doing my duty. And—I promise—I'll make it as easy as I can.

CHIPS. That's right. A bit of skirt—a lot of tears and there's another good bailiff gone West !

WIDOW (*to bailiff*). Will you stand there and let that cut-throat insult a poor defenceless widow-woman ? You wretch !

EGG (*to widow*). I won't, mum. (*To* CHIPS)—Now look here——

(*Enter* ODOROUS EGG. *The* WIDOW *ceases crying on beholding a female antagonist.*)

(*Aside*).) My sister ! Now we're for it !

ODOR. Good morning, Widow Twankey. I see that I have arrived just in time.

WIDOW (*shortly*). In time for what ?

ODOR. In time to collect that little debt before the law steps in. Just a small matter of thirty—Jimmy-o'—I mean, golden sovereigns.

WIDOW. And what do you think I'm going to use for money ? I haven't got thirty pence much less thirty pounds.

ODOR. I am not interested in the means of payment or in any of your troubles. I merely wish to collect my debt.

CHIPS (*echoing*). She meahly wishes to collect her debt. (*Bus.*)

EGG (*to* ODOR.). Sister dear, don't be hard on Widow Twankey. She's just had a bad shock. Can't you leave your business until another day ? I'm sure she'll pay you as soon as possible.

ODOR. I've been waiting for fifteen years. I think it's long enough.

CHIPS. Give the old girl a chance, Odor. Just another fifteen years !

ODOR. (*icily*). Since when have you had the privilege of directing my financial operations or of using my Christian name ? Remember your place, my man.

WIDOW (*movingly*). But, Miss Egg, I can't pay you now. Give me a little time and persuade your brother to go away, and I'll repay you. Have a little mercy !

ODOR. No !

EGG. Have mercy !

ODOR. No !

CHIPS. Mercy !

WIDOW.
EGG.
CHIPS } (*Singing*) Have mer-her-her-her-her-see !

ODOR. NO ! . . . Yes !

(*All check.*)

I will have mercy ! I'll be more than merciful ! I'll be magnanimous !

CHIPS. She'll be magnificent—magniloquent—magnesia—she'll be—eh ?

OTHERS. Yes ?

ODOR. I'll leave the debt ! I'll send the bailiff away ! I'll even pay your other debts—IF—— !

WIDOW. Pinch me—I'm dreaming ! If what, dear lady

ODOR. IF !

OTHERS (*in desperation*). If WHAT ?

ODOR. If your son Jack marries me !

(*All react, and stagger, moaning.*)

Think ! Think well what it means to you, Widow Twankey !

CHIPS (*aside*). Think what it means to Jack ! (*Groans and bus.*)

WIDOW (*pacing up and down*). Yes ! He shall marry you ! I don't know which is coming off worse, but I'll be rid of a lazy son and a packet of debts at one go ! Yes, he shall marry you ! (*Waves them upstage.*) Go and call him !

(*They all hang over the fence and call* " Jack ! " *Enter* JACK *at P.S. He comes down.*)

JACK. Hello, mother darling ! D'you want me ?

WIDOW. Yes, Jack my dearest boy, I do. (*Up to him at C. The others come down R. and L. of them.*) The bailiffs are in for the rent. I owe Miss Egg thirty pounds I can't pay, so I'm to be sold up and sent to the wukkus ! (*She struggles with grief.*) But Miss Egg, dear, sweet, beautiful Miss Egg has offered to settle everything—on one condition !

JACK (*to* ODOR.). Now isn't that nice of you ! (*To* WIDOW) What's the condition ?

WIDOW (*gulps, then smiles at him coyly*). That you marry her.

JACK (*reacting*). What ! Me ? Good lord ! *Me*—marry *that* ? Mother ! You must be mad !

ODOR. How dare you !

EGG. That's done it !

CHIPS. That's torn it !

WIDOW. You mean you'll see me in the workhouse first ?

JACK. You'll see me in my grave first !

WIDOW (*weeping*). A-a-ah ! I never thought my own son would see me go to the wukkus ! A-a-a-ah ! You'll be sorry for this one day . . . A-a-a-a-ah !

EGG.
CHIPS. } (*Chanting on one long note.*) A-a-a-a- ah!

JACK (*to them*) Shut up ! (*To* WIDOW) Oh mother, I'd do anything but this ! I'll look after the cow and the chickens ! I'll run the errands . . . I'll do my algebra—I'd even go to work ! But marry that—that old crow—HA !

EGG. HA ! (*Claps his hand over his mouth.*)

CHIPS (*artificial, falsetto laugh*). Ha-ha-ha-ha-ha-ha ! (*Checks, then softly*) Ha !

ODOR. (*to C. with a wave of the arm*). I'll not stay to be insulted by a pauper ! (*To* WIDOW). I want my money by this time tomorrow, or else . . . (*To gate and turns.*) . . . or ELSE . . .

WIDOW (*wailing*). Ow—naow !

ODOR. Pah !

(*Exits.*)

CHIPS (*quickly*). Pooh ! Jack my boy, you said a few words too many that time . . . (*Cackles with laughter.*) " Old Crow " !

(WIDOW *goes down R., and sits.*)

JACK. So she is, Chips, and you know it.

EGG. She's my sister—and don't *I* know it !

CHIPS. Maybe, but she's got a well-lined nest. You could have worse.

JACK. If you are so attracted why don't you marry her ?

CHIPS (*thinking*). Eh ? But that wouldn't do you any good.

JACK. Wouldn't it ? If you married her *I* couldn't! And *you'd* have her *money*.

CHIPS. That's an idea ! I'll try it ! You may be a *trifle* more good looking, but have you my *glamour* ? (*Goes up.*) Miss Odor ! Miss Odor !

(*Exit.*)

JACK. Good luck, Chips.

EGG. Good luck ! Good luck !

(*They wave to him, off.*)

WIDOW. Good luck indeed ! It's me that wants the luck. What are we going to do now ? (*Rises, to R.C.*)

JACK (*coming down C.*). We must pay Odorous somehow. Haven't we got *any* money ? Can't we *sell* something ?

WIDOW. We haven't anything worth selling.

JACK. Yes, we have. What about the cow ?

WIDOW. What ! Claribelle the cow ? We can't sell her ! What should we do for milk ?

EGG. Join the co-op.

JACK. Shut up. (*To* WIDOW). If we don't sell her the bailiff will and we shan't get that money.

WIDOW. Oh, to think of parting with Claribelle ! My dear sweet faithful friend, my help-meet, counsellor and guide for so many years ! When I was ill she nursed me, when I was troubled she comforted me, if I was down and out she gave me shelter, when I was hungry and thirsty she succoured me. We have been everything to each other, just like Flanagan and Allen. (*Or topical gag.*) And now—she goes.

(*She has gradually come to weep and now all three are crying. Bus. ad lib.*)

JACK. Oh, mother !
EGG. Oh, mum ! } (*All howl and wail like a siren.*)

WIDOW. All clear ! Go . . . get her and take her away before I break down.

JACK. Yes, mother.

(*Exit.*)

WIDOW. Oh, Mister*egg* !

EGG. Oh, Mrs. *Twankey* !

(*Bus. They break apart as* JACK *returns with cow. They all crowd round* CLARIBELLE *at C.*)

WIDOW. Goodbye, Claribelle, good-bye.

JACK. Good-bye—good-bye !

EGG. Bye-bye ! Bye-bye !

WIDOW. Good-bye for ever.

ALL (*singing*). Good-bye for ever. Good-bye ! Good-bye !

(CLARIBELLE *lifts up her head and sobs.* WIDOW TWANKEY *wipes cow's eyes with a garment from the clothes basket, kneeling C., below the cow.* JACK *and* EGG *lean their elbows on the cow's back, R., and L., and wipe their eyes.*)

CURTAIN.

If necessary during scene change—

WIDOW TWANKEY *in front of tabs for reprise of refrain No. 2.*

Act I. Scene 2.

Scene.—*The Road to Market.*

Setting: *Back cloth. Tree wings PS. and O.P. Bush ground row L.C., tree trunk down R.C.*

(*Enter P.S., various villagers, pedlars, and so on, singing a chorus, as they go to market.*)

(*Type of chorus,* " Hi ! Ho ! " *from* " Snow-white ")

During this, an Old Lady *threads in and out wearily, stumbling as she is pushed aside. All gradually exeunt, O.P., the* Old Lady *last.*)

No. 3. (*Chorus of Villagers and others.*)

(*Enter* Jack *leading the cow* Claribelle.)

Jack (*wiping brow*). Phew, it is hot. Come along, Claribelle—(*sighs*)—only another five miles.

Cow (*mournfully*). Moo . . . oo . . . oo.

Jack. Poor old girl. It is a shame to sell you after all these years. Do you mind *very* much ?

Cow. Moo . . . oo.

Jack. I do hope we find a good home and a kind master for you.

(Cow *reacts.*)

I don't want to sell you to someone who won't appreciate you and treat you well.

Cow (*in tears*). Moo . . . oo . . . oo.

Jack. Oh Claribelle darling, don't cry like that. You make me feel so mean. I know it's my fault that we've got to sell you. It's all my fault. We shouldn't be in such a fix if it wasn't. Oh ! (*Stamps foot.*) I know I'm lazy and stupid and mean. Expecting everything and giving nothing. I'm no good to anybody. (*Pause, then with sudden resolution.*) Claribelle, I'm going to take you back and I'm going to marry Odorous. It's time I made some sacrifice.

Cow (*loudly protesting*). Moo . . . Moo . . . Moo !

Jack (*surprised*). What ! You don't want me to ?

COW (*decisively*). Moo !

JACK. But you'll have a warm dry shed and as much lovely sweet smelling hay as you want. Mother won't have any debts and I—I shall have a rich wife.

COW (*angrily*). Moo ! Moo ! Moo ! (*Stamping feet.*)

JACK (*warmly*). Bless you, you old darling. You know I'd hate to marry her and you're going to sacrifice yourself to save me (*Embraces and kisses cow.*)

(*Appropriate actions by cow on being kissed.*)

No. 4. *Song and Dance* (JACK and CLARIBELLE.)

(*After dance enter the* OLD LADY, *L.*, JACK, *who is embracing the cow, hastily releases her, on seeing the* OLD LADY.)

JACK (*surprised*). Oh ! . . . You must think I'm silly kissing a cow. I don't make a habit of it. This is a special occasion because——

(*His voice trails off as the* OLD LADY, *who has taken little notice sits wearily on a tree stump.*)

You do look tired. Have you come far ?

OLD LADY. From—— (*Local town.*)

JACK. ——? In this heat and dust? You must be worn out.

OLD LADY. I am. But I've got to be at —— (*Local town.*) before the market finishes or I won't get work.

JACK. Work ? Do you have to work ?

(ODOR. *and* CHIPS *enter P.S. and hide behind the bush.* CHIPS *would hail* JACK *but* ODOR. *prevents him.*)

OLD LADY. If I don't work, I don't eat.

JACK. But haven't you any money or relations ?

OLD LADY. Nothing.

JACK. Oh ! (*Puts hand into pocket and brings out money.*) Here, take this tuppence. It's all I've got but I shan't need it.

OLD LADY. No. Oh, no ! I couldn't do that.

JACK. Please ! I'm ashamed I can't give you more but it's all I have. (*Aside*). That is, except Claribelle (*Pauses and thinks.*) Yes—yes. (*To* OLD LADY). You can have Claribelle.

OLD LADY (*puzzled*). Claribelle ?

JACK. The cow.

OLD LADY. The cow ? What good will a cow be to me ?

JACK. You can sell her when you get to market and perhaps the farmer that buys her will hire you as well.

OLD LADY (*gratefully*). Oh, my dear, it's so kind of you, so kind of you. But what will your mother say when you get back ?

JACK (*doubtfully*). I—I—I'll explain it to her. She'll understand. Won't she, Claribelle ?

COW (*who seems quite content*). Moo ! (*Dances two or three short steps.*)

JACK. There, Claribelle is quite happy about it.

OLD LADY. Then I'll take her, dear boy. But I must give you something in exchange. (*She gives* JACK *a small cloth bag.*) Here, this is for you, with all my thanks.

JACK (*taking bag*). Why—Thank you. (*He looks inside.*) But—(*He laughs.*)—there's nothing in here but a few beans. (*Handing bag back.*) I can't take these.

OLD LADY. Yes, yes, you must !

JACK. Oh, no, I——

OLD LADY (*fiercely*). Yes, yes, keep them I say—keep them !

JACK (*soothingly*). Very well and—er—er—thank you.

OLD LADY. That's right. And now I will get on my way. You are a good boy and my blessings go with you. Look after my gift and you'll find your heart's desire. Don't forget me. Good-bye ! (*To R.C. leading cow and turns.*) Remember ! Look after my gift ! (*Exits R.*)

JACK. I will! Good-bye! . . . What a queer old creature. (*He remembers, looks at the bag and laughs*)—beans! (*Grows solemn.*) Beans! That's what I'm to get when mother hears about it! (*Exit L.*)

(ODOR. *and* CHIPS *come out of hiding.*)

ODOR. The lazy good-for-nothing! Giving the cow away because he's too lazy to walk to market.

CHIPS. No, Odorous. He was sorry for her, that's why. He's that tender hearted—you wouldn't believe!

ODOR. He's a fool—and you're a bigger one. No wonder you support him!

CHIPS. But, Odorous——

ODOR. And don't call me Odorous! As for Jack—oh, I could—— (*Clenches her teeth.*)

CHIPS. You don't seem to like him.

ODOR. Like him? Like him? I scorn and despise him.

CHIPS (*brightening up*). Then if you don't like him any more how about—er—how about—you——

ODOR. Don't gibber, man. What is wrong with you?

CHIPS. Well, I—er—I—ooer—— (*Makes noise as if in pain and then drops on his knees.*)

ODOR. Aren't you well? What is wrong? (*She moves away.* CHIPS *on his knees follows.*)

CHIPS. I—oh, oh, Odor—please, I want to——

ODOR. Mercy! He's foaming at the mouth (*She shrieks.*) You're mad. You've got hydrophobia. (*She shrieks again and backs away.*)

CHIPS (*emotionally*). Odorous! Oh, Odorous Egg, I——I (*As she backs away,* CHIPS, *still on his knees, makes a grab at her round the knees and brings her down.*)—I love you. Will you marry me? (*Louder.*) Will you marry me? (*Shouts in her ear.*) Will you marry me?

(ODOROUS *sits up abruptly.*)

ODOR. What! Marry you! You're mad! (*Scrambling up.*) What gives you *that* idea? (*Goes into hysterical laughter and clouts* CHIPS.) Eh? What makes you think I'd marry you, you moth-eaten, bald-headed bag of . . . eh ?

CHIPS. Well, you said you'd finished with Jack ! So if you don't marry him what *are* you going to do ?

ODOR. Do ? What's *he* going to do when he gets home with only a bag of beans ? What's his mother going to do ? Come on ! Back to the cottage for a real reit *do* ! (*Runs off L.*)

CHIPS (*Following*). Odor ! Wait a minute—(*Checks.*) No ! Why should I ? No woman can turn me down with impu—imper—impun—intup—anyway, I haven't done me singing practice ! (*Goes into* :—)

No. 5. *Song* ... ... (CHIPS)

CURTAIN.

END OF SCENE 2.

During scene change, CHIPS, *having sung one verse and refrain, comes down in front of tabs, for second verse, and the refrain, which he teaches to the audience.*

Act I. Scene 3.

Scene—*The Cottage Garden.*

The Widow *is pacing up and down (across stage) anxiously. Now and then she goes through the fence gate and looks down the road.* Jack *appears left but he is afraid to face his mother. (Business of this while she stands C. facing the audience).)*

Widow. How much longer will he be ? It's time he was back. I'm all of a dither. I wonder how much he got for her ? Poor Claribelle ! I'll never have another like her. Never mind ! If he got what she was worth, I'll be able to square Odorous and have a little left over. I hope he doesn't get robbed or get mixed up with those (*Local town*) girls. Oh dear (*Agitated*)—I should have sent someone with him. It's very likely that he . . .

(*Here* Jack *tiptoes up behind her and puts one hand over her eyes.*)

(*She screams.*) Oh—oh—who is it ?

Jack. I'll give you one guess, mother. (*Takes his hand away and they face each other.*)

Widow. Jack ! I'm so glad you're back. I was having terrible thoughts about you. (*She sees bag.*) Oh ! (*Delighted.*) Did you get all that for Claribelle ? There must be at least fifty sovereigns there. I knew I could rely on you, Jack, my darling, my clever, clever darling.

Jack. But—mother——

Widow (*taking no notice*). Not that she wasn't worth every penny of it. Let me see the lovely shining gold that is going to save us from Odorous and the workhouse !

Jack. But, mother, listen . . .

(*The* Widow *does not heed him and takes the bag, weighing it in her hands and showing great delight at its heaviness.*)

WIDOW. I've never had so much money in my hands before. It gives me such a lovely warm feeling. Just like a gin and pep. Let me hear it jingle. (*She shakes bag by her ear. Surprised, she shakes harder.*) Not very loud. I suppose it's too heavy to make a noise. I'll open it, and let it run through my fingers.

JACK (*backing away, dithering*). Mother ! Mother !

(*Smiling, the* WIDOW *opens bag and puts her hands in. Then she shows surprise, amazement, unbelief, and finally anger.*)

WIDOW (*screams*). What's this ? What's this ?

JACK (*frightened*). B—B—B—Beans, mother !

WIDOW. Beans ? Beans ? BEANS ? Ooh-er ! (*She breaks down and cries uncontrollably moving to well down L.C. and sits.*)

(JACK *is frightened, but after a time he goes to her to comfort her.*)

JACK. I'm sorry, so sorry, mother. I didn't think.

WIDOW (*flinging his arm off as rage takes the place of tears*). Think ? Didn't think ! (*Springs up and pushes him away.*) You haven't got anything to think *with* ! Beans ! Bah ! (*Flings the beans over the garden.*) There go your beans and you can go with them, and never let me see your face again. (*She pushes him away violently and goes into the cottage slamming the door after her.*)

(JACK *goes and knocks on door frantically.*)

JACK. Mother, mother, let me in . . . Please, oh please. (*Knocks again.*) Oh, mother—(*in tears*)—mother ! Mother ! Mother, let me in ! Oh do let me in—I'm ever so sorry, really I am . . .

WIDOW. You're not coming in here ! You can stop out all night !

JACK. Mother—I'll make it up to you—I promise I will . . .

WIDOW. Go AWAY ! Go and drown yourself in the well . . .

JACK. I might as well. (*Turning away.*) Oh, isn t it awful ? No money—no Claribelle—no bed—no supper . . . Oh-o-oh !

(*He breaks down and goes to the garden seat and stretches himself out, sobbing.* ODOROUS *creeps in above the wall laughing silently, and shaking her fist.*)

(*She exits.*)

(*And the lights begin to fade.* JACK *closes his eyes, as soft music plays. Five fairies enter from behind the tree and dance round him as he sleeps. They are followed by colour wheel.*)

No. 6 ... ... *Dance of the Fairies.*

(*The* BEANSTALK BEGINS TO GROW, *up stage at L. corner of the cottage. There is light only on the garden seat, the beanstalk, and the fairies. They retreat and exeunt R. and L., as lights fade to nil. See* LIGHTING PLOT.)

END OF SCENE 3.

(*Soft music continues during B.O. while the beanstalk is drawn up—curtain falls if necessary—and fades out as Sc. 4 lighting fades in.*)

Act I. Scene 4.

Scene—*The Cottage Garden.*

(*Lighting fades in to dawn effect.*)

(Jack *remains asleep. Enter* Odorous *at the garden gate. She looks at* Jack, *grins, and goes to cottage door and knocks quietly, then steps back a pace.* Widow Twankey *opens the door.*)

Widow (*pessimistically*). Oh ! It's you, is it ?

Odor. Yes, it is ! I've come for my money.

Widow. Oh ?—Er—yes. Will you come in ?

Odor. No. I'll remain here. I'm in a hurry.

Widow. Then I'll . . but—er . . . as a matter of fact . . .

Odor. As a matter of fact, you haven't got the money, have you ?

Widow. How do you know ?

Odor. Because I saw him sell the cow to an old scarecrow of a woman. And he sold it for a bag of beans.

Widow. He *sold* Claribelle for those beans ? (*Comes down R.C.*) O-o-oh ! The worthless, good-for-nothing, idle, brainless, lazy, stupid, sinful, useless . . .

Odor. (*Down on L. of* Widow, *R.C.*) I know all about him so you needn't tell me his history. I'm not interested. But what I am interested in is how you are going to pay me. Eh ? I'd like to know that

Widow. So would I ! So would I ! I haven't even got the price of a pint . . ow ! (*She throws her apron over her head and howls*).

Odor. Stop that, you old wreck ! That won't help you.

(Widow *stops at word* " wreck " *and uncovers her face.*)

Widow. Don't call me an old wreck, you old crow. (*Moves menacingly to* Odor. *who backs to L.C.*) If crying won't help perhaps you'll tell me what will ?

ODOR. (*flinching at words* "old crow"). I will. Listen, horse-face. Jack isn't very pleased with life now. He's feeling sorry for himself, isn't he ? Nowhere to go, no friends, no money.

WIDOW (*C.*). That's true . . . caustic features.

ODOR. Then here's your chance to make him marry me and save yourself from the workhouse.

WIDOW. I'd marry him to (*Topical name*) if it would save me going to the spike.

ODOR. Good. Wake him up and let us get it settled before you become reconciled to the idea of workhouse Christmas pudding.

WIDOW. Reconciled ! Never ! Come along.

They move to where JACK *is sleeping. The* WIDOW *shakes him as* ODOROUS *views him with marked satisfaction.*)

Wake up, Jack. Wake up, you——

(ODOR. *puts her finger to her lips.*)

ODOR. (*L. of seat*). Hush ! You mustn't upset him.

WIDOW (*R. of seat*). Jack (*Snarls.*) my dear boy, wake up.

(ODOR. *bends over him as he gradually wakes and stretches.*)

JACK (*making waking up noises and half sitting up*). What a nightmare ! I dreamt I was married to Odorous and on the honeymoon—(*He stops as he sees* ODOR.). Oh ! I thought I was awake but I'm still asleep and Stinker's still there. (*He lies back again.*)

WIDOW. You are awake. (*Rolls him off the seat.*) And as for dreaming you were married to Odorous . . . you were having good practice. For marry her you will and before the day's out. I'll give you sell Claribelle for a handful of beans. (*She picks up a stick and is about to belabour him but* ODOR. *checks her.*)

(JACK *scrambles to his feet.*)

JACK. I'm sorry about Claribelle, mother, but . . . (*Backing away.*)

WIDOW (*advancing on him*). You'll be sorrier when you're married.

JACK. I won't marry her.

WIDOW. (*Same bus.*) I'll show you.

JACK (*still retreating*). No, no! I won't marry her. Wild horses wouldn't drag me to it.

WIDOW. No? But your mother and intended will. Catch him, Odor.

(*They grab at* JACK *who eludes them and business of chase follows. While this goes on* EGG *and* CHIPS *enter, who remain on road side of gate and shout encouragement impartially. This may be gagged* ad lib. *The beanstalk has remained unnoticed but suddenly* JACK *sees it.*)

JACK. Ah! A beanstalk. And what a beanstalk!

(EGG *and* CHIPS *come down into the garden.*)

WIDOW (*seeing beanstalk*). Mercy—look at it!

ODOR. Something's happened—it's magic—Eggy!

EGG. Scarlet Runner! (*Together with bus.* ad lib. *as* JACK *climbs, unnoticed by them.*)

CHIPS. S'crimson rambler!

JACK Bye-bye! (*Disappears at head of beanstalk.*)

(*The others make a rush for the beanstalk, colliding and shouting.*)

ODOR. Egg!—Chips! Fetch him! He shan't escape me . . . (*Climbs three or four steps.*)

WIDOW (*wringing her hands*). Oh, do something! Do something!

CHIPS. Fetch a plumber! Get off me foot!

EGG. Call the Fire Brigade! That's my stomach!

(ODOR. *falls on the* WIDOW, *who knocks over* EGG *and* CHIPS. *A general collision and mêlée.*)

(*When they have picked themselves up*:)

ODOR.
WIDOW } (*Together.*) You've got to get Jack back!

EGG. Jack back?

CHIPS. What a crack!

WIDOW (*to* ODOR.). Then *you* go!

ODOR. I'm too weak! I couldn't climb!

WIDOW. Nonsense! You're not going to let Jack get away, are you?

(ODOR. *feebly shakes her head.*)

Well then, up with you. (*Pulls* ODOR. *up*) Now, Mr. Egg, you carry her up that beanstalk.

EGG (*nervous*). Up there? . . . Oh no, I couldn't, I daren't! Why not wait for him to come down?

WIDOW. He won't while she's here . . . and can you blame him?

ODOR. Eh?

WIDOW. She's got to follow him and you've got to take her.

EGG. No! No! No! I've no head for heights . . . I daren't!

WIDOW. (*Coy.*) Oh, Mr. Egg! Not to please *me*?

EGG. Well—er—er——

WIDOW. There's a curly headed boy. (*To* ODOR.) Come on, you! On his back!

CHIPS. Any more for the "skylark"! (*Gags* ad lib.)

(*Business of* ODOR. *on* EGG'S *back*, WIDOW *and* CHIPS *helping. They try twice to climb but fall both times*)

EGG. (*Gasping*) It's no good. I can't do it.

(CHIPS *goes down L. and sits on well. Turns wheel like a barrel organ and holds out hat. Business.*)

ODOR. Nor me either. I'm....

WIDOW. (*Anxiously*) Fiddlesticks! I'd never let a beanstalk stand between me and a man. (*She looks round*) Here, try Chips, your brother's no good. Come on Chips!

CHIPS. (*Bus singing*) "Kind, kind and gentle is she...."

ODOR. Chips! Transport me up that beanstalk!

CHIPS. What! No, I ain't got me passenger carrying licence yet.

ODOR. Don't quibble. Come here!

CHIPS. Not bloomin' likely.

WIDOW (*aside to* EGG.) Grab him.

(*Another chase ensues around the well and ends by* CHIPS *slowly climbing with* ODOR. *on his back.*)

EGG (*waving*). Good-luck ! Goo'-bye.

WIDOW (*waving*). Send us a post card ! Give me love to George ! (*As* ODOR *and* CHIPS *disappear she smiles coyly at* EGG.) Thank you for helping me Mr. Egg. it was good of you, reellee !

(*Coy glances at each other.*)

EGG. Not at all. I . . . I'd do anything for you, Widow Twankey.

WIDOW (*coyly*). Would you, reelly ? Oh, I say ! . . . (*Sharply.*) Good ! Then get up there and save my poor Jack from your sister—there you are—that's what you can do . . .

EGG. Oh, but look here, I didn't say I'd——

WIDOW. You said " anything "—and this is something . . . (*Pushes him towards beanstalk.*) Oh, Eggy darling, all for your little Twankey-wankey . . . (*Kisses his bald head.*) Oh, aren't I a forward *thing* ! (*Hoisting him up.*) Oopsy-day !

EGG (*climbing*). I feel sick ! What do I do when I get there ?

WIDOW. BRING BACK JACK ! (*Waving, as curtain falls.*) Goo'-bye ! Goo'-bye ! Goo'-bye!

CURTAIN.

END OF ACT I.

ACT II.

SCENE I.

SCENE.—*The Road to the Castle.*

(*A short* " *Fairy Chorus* " *may be sung, softly,* off stage, *as curtain rises.*)

As the curtain rises (*to music*) *the lighting fades in—moonlight to dawn, as the* FAIRIES *enter, either O.P., or through cuts in the cloth. They are dancing, and go from R. to L., and up C., then retreat with beckoning gestures, drawing* JACK *on from C., through cut in cloth.*

JACK *gives no sign of being aware of the* FAIRIES' *presence. His expression is one of bewilderment. The* FAIRIES *exeunt, dancing, and the music fades out.*

JACK (*coming down stage*). What a place ! There's something funny about it ! I feel as if there were people all round me—but there's no one ! Not a man, woman, child, bird, or beast to be seen. (*Sits.*) And no adventure after all. Being hungry and tired and lonely isn't an adventure—I'm starving. (*Rises and shouts.*) Hey ! Anyone round here ?

ECHO (*off*). . . . round here ? (JACK *hears thus, and reacts.*)

JACK. Round where ?

ECHO (*off*). . . . 'dwhere !

JACK (*shouting*). I want some *dinner* !

ECHO (*off*). . . . some dinner !

JACK. Don't keep repeating—it's so *rude* !

ECHO (*off—softly, then rising like a howl of wind*). Ru-u-u-u-u-u-u-ude ! (*Flash, clap of thunder.*)

JACK (*frightened*). That's done it ! I'm off ! I'm going home !

(*Fairies laughter off.*)

Don't laugh at me—I'm going home !

(*Long wailing sigh of* " Ho . . . ome " !

Ow! I'd rather face mother and Odorous too . . . (*Goes L.*)

OLD LADY (*entering R.*). No! Don't do that!

JACK (*spinning round*). What!

OLD LADY. I say—don't—do—*that*!

JACK. Wh—why! You're the old—the old lady who had Claribelle, aren't you? How did you get here?

OLD LADY. I'm all over the place—(*Laughs queerly.*)—I'm never very far away from anywhere!

JACK (*puzzled*). Oh! Where's Claribelle?

OLD LADY. Oh, she's in very good hands and quite contented—not like her young master, eh?

JACK. No! I thought I'd find adventure here, but there's nothing but funny noises. I—er—I was just going back!

OLD LADY. And I—said—no! I don't want to see you give in, after I've helped you to escape from that Odorous woman!

JACK. You *helped* me to escape?

OLD LADY (*laughing queerly*). Well, you *climbed my beanstalk*, didn't you?

JACK (*suddenly remembering*). Oh yes! Those beans you gave me! Marvellous! I've never seen anything like them!

OLD LADY. Little wonder . . .

JACK. I should have said "Giant Wonder."

OLD LADY. Giant! You may well say that! You don't know where you are, do you?

JACK. N—no!

OLD LADY. You're in Megalomania—the Land of the Giant Snufflegobbler.

JACK. Snufflegobbler? Never heard of him!

OLD LADY (*pointing off R.*). That's his castle—just beyond that hill (*laughs*). You'll find all the adventure you want there! Oh yes—all the adventure any boy could want! Think of it! A real Giant!

JACK. Oh—er—really? Is it safe?

OLD LADY. (*Snorts.*) Safe! Is any adventure safe? Are you afraid?

JACK. Yes. (*Gulps.*)—but—(*Smiles.*)—I'm going—(*Stares front as* OLD LADY *retreats and exits quietly.*)—I *know*—I *must* go ! (*Turning.*) But will you tell me . . . goodness ! She's gone !

(*Fairies dance on L., behind Jack, making passes in the air that seem to propel him forward to R.*)

And I must go too ! The Giant's Castle ! And my adventure.

(JACK *exits.* FAIRIES *turn at R.C. to face L. Suddenly all stand quite still. Then, exeunt with little cries and laughter—if possible through cuts in the back-cloth—as sounds of quarrelling is heard off L.*)

(*Enter* ODOROUS, EGG, *and* CHIPS, *L.* ODOROUS' *dress is torn, her hair untidy.* CHIPS *has torn trousers, etc.,* EGG *is also exhausted.*)

ODOROUS (*to* CHIPS). You disgusting beast !

CHIPS (*to* EGG). You clumsy twirp !

EGG. Clumsy twirp ! Look at my hand !

CHIPS. How did I know you were going to put it under my foot ?

ODOROUS (*to* CHIPS). And why must you tear half my clothes off ? What do you think I am ? A strip tease act ?

CHIPS. I had to grab someone !

ODOROUS. Why pick on me ? (*Pushes him on top of* EGG.)

EGG. Why tread on *me* ?

CHIPS (*recovering*). I might have broken my neck !

ODOR. *and* EGG (*together*). What a good idea !

ODOR. (*to* EGG). You needn't butt in ! What are you doing coming up here, anyway ?

EGG. Well—er—Widow Twankey asked me to !

ODOROUS. Why ?

EGG. Because she wanted me to !

ODOR. Why ?

EGG. Because she likes me ! (*Coy bus. and giggles.*)

ODOR. *and* CHIPS (*mocking echo*). Because she likes me ! (*To each other.*) You shut up !

CHIPS (*to* EGG). Gr-r-r-r-!

ODOROUS. That's enough! Back you go, Egg! Back to your job and see that old scraggy-necked widow doesn't flit! You'll be lucky if she hasn't already gone!

EGG. Oh, she wouldn't do that!

ODOR. *and* CHIPS. WHY?

ALL THREE (*together*). Because she likes me!

ODOROUS (*to* CHIPS). That's enough, you! (*To* EGG.) If you aren't gone in two seconds I'll stop your pocket money again!

EGG. Ow naow! Not again!

ODOROUS. Yes! Again!

EGG. Oh you are unki-i-i-ind! I must have some pocket money!

ODOROUS. Why?

EGG *and* CHIPS. BECAUSE SHE LIKES ME . . . (CHIPS *pushes* EGG *off. He tumbles head over heels and disappears behind L. tree flat.*)

ODOROUS. That's settled him! Come on you! We'll follow the road and find Jack . . . (*She drags* CHIPS *off R.*)

(*The* FAIRIES *peep out and watch* EGG *re-enter and cross scout fashion and exit R. Then* FAIRIES *go into a very short, spirited dance, ending in a sudden B.O., green flash, and B.O. again as the curtain falls.*)

(*During scene change,* WIDOW TWANKEY *in front of tabs* :—)

No. 7. *Patter Song* ... WIDOW TWANKEY.

END OF SCENE I.

ACT II. SCENE 2.

SCENE.—*The Kitchen of Giant Snufflegobbler's Castle.*

(*Entrance up L.C. Doorway R. Window L.*)

(JILL *is on stage looking unhappy, dressed in rags, sweeping and singing.*)

No. 8 *Song* ... ... JILL

Exit at end of song.

JACK. (*Off.*) Is anyone there ? . . . (*Knocks.*) May I come in ? (*Knocks.*)

(*Enter* JACK *up L.C.*)

Well . . . I'm *in* ! (*Walks around examining room. Calls.*) Anyone at home ? . . . What a queer looking place. I don't altogether like this. I'll have to watch my step . . . a-ah !

(*Staggers back as he hears crash. And noises off—saucepan lids, etc.*)

Gosh ! What's that ? Th-th-the Giant ?—I'd better hide. (*He hides quickly behind R. of doorway up L.C.*)

(*Enter* JILL *carrying table cloth. Goes to table C., lays cloth.*)

(*Peeping out.*) It's a girl . . . (*Enthusiastically.*) It's a beautiful girl ! *She* can't do me any harm !
(*He preens himself and steps out of his hiding place.*) Er—excuse me—er——

(JILL *turns and drops back in fright.*)

JILL (*scared*). Oh . . . Oh . . . Who are you ? What are you doing here ?

JACK. I've lost my way and I'm hungry and thirsty. So when I saw this castle, I decided to ask for something to eat and drink, and to find out where I was.

JILL (*in panic*). But you can't stay here. Don't you know who lives here ?

JACK. Who ?

JILL. Giant Snufflegobbler !

JACK (*boldly*). Oh yes—I've heard of him ! Well ! What about it ? Surely he'd give a hungry traveller something to eat ?

JILL. Yes. He'd give you as much to eat as you liked for a week or so and . . .

JACK. That sounds all right !

JILL. . . . and then . . .

JACK. And then ?

JILL. He—he'd eat you himself !

JACK (*astonished*). Eat me ? Why ?

JILL. He eats boys and girls. Especially English nes. He says they are . . . they're prime.

JACK. I don't think I shall like him, somehow (*Shudder,—pause.*) Why hasn't he eaten *you* ?

JILL. He says I'm too useful in the house, and anyway he says I'm too skinny.

JACK. Skinny ? You're not. I think you're just right.

JILL (*shyly*). Do you ?

JACK. I think you're *lovely* !

JILL. Do you really ? What is " lovely " ?

JACK. Well—er—it's sort of—I mean, I like looking at you ! . . . What's your name ?

JILL. Jill.

JACK. Jill what ?

JILL. I don't know.

JACK. You don't know your other name ? That's strange.

JILL. Not really. You see, when I was about four the Giant stole me and I was too tiny to remember my surname.

JACK. Then how do you know your name is Jill ?

JILL. Because when I was stolen I had a brooch on my dress and I've still got it. See, it has my name on it.

JACK (*lookimg at brooch*). Jill . . . and a crown above it . . . it can't be that . . . No ! It's impossible ! (*Stares at her.*) Oh, I'm not going *now* !

JILL. But you *mustn't* stay ! The Giant will be back for dinner soon.

JACK. Surely you're not going to send me away without anything to eat ?

JILL. I must ! I tell you he'll eat you if he catches you.

JACK (*appealing*). Jill !

(JILL *appears undecided as she is obviously impressed by* JACK.)

(*Appealing.*) Jill ! . . . Darling !

(*She smiles.*)

JILL. All right then. But we must hurry. (*To cupboard for cake and milk.*) Er—what is *your* name ? (*Puts the food before him.*)

JACK. Jack. (*Sits L. of table.*)

JILL (*standing above table*). And your other name ?

JACK. Twankey. But you call me Jack because I can only call you Jill . . . darling !

(*She pours some milk for* JACK *who drinks.*)

JILL. Very well, Jack—(*Pause and she smiles roguishly.*)—darling !

JACK (*pleased*). That sounded better than I've ever heard it sound before.

JILL. Oh, did it ? . . . What does it mean ?

JACK (*disappointed*). Oh ! I thought you knew . . . it means . . . it means that you like me.

No. 9. *Duet* ... ... JACK *and* JILL.

JILL. (*After number.*) Well, if you've finished, I'll show you your way from the castle walls.

JACK. But, Jill ! I'm still tired. Can't I stay a little longer ?

JILL. You must be gone before the Giant returns. If we go to the walls we shall see him approach. Come, Jack.

(*She takes his hand and both exit, singing final phrases of duet refrain.*)

(*Enter* ODOR *and* CHIPS.)

CHIPS. Lummy ! What a country ! Not a pub for miles and me with a thirst you could chop up and sell for salt.

ODOR. Don't be vulgar ! And don't stand there snivelling. This, apparently, is a kitchen. There's sure to be something to drink here. Look for something ! Look for something.

CHIPS. O.K., Toots.

(CHIPS, *bus. darting here and there, peering in corners, under table and so on.* ODOR. *follows—bus. and collisions.*)

(CHIPS *comes to a cupboard, up R., opens it and finds several bottles. He looks at them and finally hands one to* ODOR *who is now behind him. She takes it and drinks. She coughs and grimaces,* ad lib.)

ODOR. (*Horror.*) Vinegar !

CHIPS. I know. I thought you always drank it !

ODOR. You villain ! I'll . . . (*She threatens him with bottle.*)

CHIPS. (*Alarm.*) 'Ere, 'ere, go easy. Who's going to carry you down if you corpse me ? We can't afford to quarrel !

No. 10. *Duet* ... ... ODOR *and* CHIPS.

(*After number, there is a knock on the door—they both scream and turn to see* EGG *come in timidly. They both react.*)

CHIPS. Look what's walked in.

ODOR. Why haven't you gone back ?

EGG. I tried to find somewhere to get a drink and got lost and . . . I didn't get a drink.

ODOR. Here's one. Try this. (*Hands him the vinegar bottle.*)

EGG (*overwhelmed*). Oh thank you, Odorous. Thank you very much, I'm sure. (*Turns away, glancing at label.*)

CHIPS. And don't drink the lot. I haven't had any yet.

EGG. Oh, no, I won't . . . but I have such a thirst. (*To* ODOR.) Have you had any ?

ODOR. I have.

EGG (*to* CHIPS). I hardly dare trust myself with this.

(*He raises bottle to drink. Business of* ODOR *and* CHIPS *watching.* EGG *pauses.*)

(*to* ODOR.). Are you sure you've had some ?

ODOR. Do you think I'd allow you to drink before me ?

EGG. No ! Well. (*He raises bottle. Then to* CHIPS.) You haven't had any yet ?

CHIPS. No. It's all right—after you.

EGG. Thank you . . . Well bung-ho . . . (*He raises bottle, business . . . and pauses.*) No . . . You had to carry Odorous. You have first drink ! Go on ! Do !

CHIPS. Oh, no, that's all right—you first.

EGG (*raising bottle*). Well, here's how . . . No, I can't. You first.

CHIPS. No ! You . . . } (*Ad lib.*)
EGG. No ! You . . . }

ODOR. (*shouting*). Quiet ! (*To* CHIPS *in a sinister voice.*) Yes . . . Oh, yes, Chips. You shall drink first. You allowed me to, so it's only right that you should now.

CHIPS. No, no !

EGG. Of course you must. (*Gives* CHIPS *the bottle.*)

ODOR. (*threatening, aside*). Go on—you mutt ! Go on, drink !

(*Business of* CHIPS *drinking, choking.*)

EGG (*delighted*). You should've done what I did, look at the label !

ODOR. I want something to eat.

CHIPS. I'll see if there's anything in the cupboard.

(EGG *and* CHIPS *look in the cupboard.*)

EGG. There's only some mouldy potatoes and an empty salmon tin. (*Brings them to table.*)

ODOR. That isn't much good.

CHIPS. Well, here's a bag of flour.

ODOR. That's better. Mouldy potatoes, a bag of flour and a salmon tin. I don't know what can be made of that.

EGG. Nay ! Here's cookery book ! (*Produces a book from the cupboard.*)

ODOR. What is it ?

EGG (*reading*). " How to get Owt from Nowt " by a Yorkshire Housewife. (*Or local gag.*)

CHIPS (*snatching book from* EGG). Let me see ! (*Opens book and reads.*) Ah ! Here's a good one. Listen ! Take two pounds of butter, four of sugar, half a pint of cream, six eggs and salt to taste . . .

ODOR. Idiot, we can't have that, we've no salt.

EGG. No salt !

CHIPS. No salt ! . . . That's torn it ! Well, how about this, " Spinster's Special " or " How to Dish Up an Old Crab."

ODOR (*angrily*). Here, give it to me ! I'll find something. (*Looks through the book.*) This'll do ! (*Reads.*) Take any of yesterday's cold potatoes, a pint of water, an empty salmon tin with a red label—(*To others.*)—red label ?

EGG. It's a blue label !

CHIPS. Dished again !

(Note : *Instead of the following dialogue, up to the entrance of* JACK *and* JILL, *a NUMBER could be introduced here, each taking one verse, and unison refrains and dance.*)

ODOR. Doesn't matter ! Blue's my colour ! (*Reading.*) Make a purée of the potatoes . . .

CHIPS. What's a purée ?

ODOR. Well—er—it's—er—it's a sort of——

EGG. It's a mess—go on.

ODOR. . . . . make a purée of the potatoes, flour, scraps and water, stir until sloppy and then pour mixture in and out of salmon tin to give added flavour. Then chop red—blue—label into small pieces and add to mixture. Cigarette and tobacco ash gives an attractive taste. Bake until brown or black if desired and serve hot, warm or cold according to the temper of the cook. Just what we wanted ! (*Plunges hands into the flour.*)

CHIPS. Ee ! It sounds grand !

(ODOR *excitedly dashes flour into his face.*)

EGG. I can smell it already.

(ODOR.—*same bus. to Egg.*)

ODOR. (*throwing up flour*). Yippee !

(*All scream and turn as* JACK *and* JILL *run on R.* ODOR., CHIPS, EGG *stagger back.*)

JILL (*horrified*). What are you doing here ? Who are you ?

EGG. Hullo, Jack !

CHIPS. Whatcher !

(ODOR. *glances at* JILL *and sniffs.*)

ODOR. Reelly ! (*Looking* JILL *up and down.*) And *who* is this young woman ?

JACK. This is Jill !

ODOR. (*to* EGG *and* CHIPS). Common.

EGG *and* CHIPS. } Oh fratefulleh! Fratefulleh !

JILL (*to* JACK). Are they with you ? Oh, dear ! Look at this disgusting mess, and the Giant will be home soon.

CHIPS. ODOR. EGG. } Giant ? (*Stagger back. Bus.*)

JACK. Yes. Don't you know you're in a *Giant's* house ?

(*Bus. repeated.*)

And a man-eater, too. (*Groans and bus.*) Get this mess cleaned up quickly.

JILL. Yes, please do.

ODOR. You're the housemaid—do it yourself ! Ay nevah soil may fingahs !

(ODOR. *remains aloof, dithering about looking nervously here and there.* JACK, JILL, EGG *and* CHIPS *clean up with many collisions, bus. and quarrelling.*)

ODOR. Out of my way !

(*Bus. collide.*)

JILL. Oh, hurry !

JACK. Don't bother her. The Giant won't fancy her. Too scraggy!

ODOR. What's that?

CHIPS. Careful! You might have to marry her yet. (*To* EGG). Get off my foot! (*Bus. collide.*)

JACK. Not likely. I'm going to marry . . .

(GIANT *approaches. Noises off.*)

JILL. He's coming! He's coming! Hide . . . oh hide . . . (*Panic.*) In the copper, Jack . . .

(JACK *hides in the copper.* EGG *and* CHIPS *under the table hidden by the table cloth which hangs well below it all round.*)

GIANT. (*Off.*) Fee-Fi-Fo-Fum!

JILL (*to* ODOR). You in that cupboard!

(ODOR *flies into cupboard.*)

GIANT. (*Sings off.*) "Fee-Fi-Fo-Fum!"

(JILL *busies herself with preparation of food, etc.*)

(*Enter* GIANT.)

GIANT. (*Singing.*)
Fee-Fi-Fo-Fum
Where is that Englishman?
Where have you hidden him?
Fee-Fi-Fo-Fim!

(*Speaking thunderously.*) Where is he, I say!

JILL. There's no one here, master. It is the lovely stew I am cooking for dinner that you can smell.

GIANT. Stew! Stew! Bah! I smell Englishman.

(*Table cloth trembles.*)

JILL. Oh, but please, it must be the stew, master. I am cooking a cow from Clapham Common (*Or local town.*)—that's why it smells English.

(*The tablecloth lifts occasionally and* EGG *and* CHIPS *look out.*)

GIANT. (*Grunts.*) Ah . . . ah . . . it may be so. It is a very disturbing smell and I don't fancy a tame stew now. (*Prowls about.*) What else have you got?

JILL. Well, master, there's . . .

GIANT. No matter. I'll have *egg*—and *chips.*

(*Consternation of* EGG *and* CHIPS, *who peep out, below table. Bus.*)

I'll have the egg fried well on both sides—in boiling fat—(EGG *disappears.*)—aha !—and the chips . . . well, see that they are sliced up thin and done slowly to a nice golden-*brown* !

(CHIPS *disappears.* GIANT *gurgles and licks his lips.*)

JILL. Yes, master. I'll get them ready immediately.

(*Tablecloth trembles violently—faint groans are heard.*)

GIANT. What was that noise ?

JILL. It was only the wind in the trees, master.

GIANT. Ah ! . . .

(EGG *and* CHIPS *stifle moans.*)

. . . What was that ?

JILL. That was the stew boiling over. (*Moving R.C.*) I must go and see to it.

GIANT. Stay !

(JILL *checks frightened, at R.C.*)

My nerves are upset by this strange smell. Bring my money-bags that I may soothe myself with those beautiful golden sovereigns.

(JILL *goes to chest and fetches bags to table.* GIANT *opens bags, pours gold out and makes animal noises over it.*)

GIANT. Lovely . . . wonderful . . . my beautiful treasure, etc. (*Ad lib.*)

(JILL *continues with housework.* EGG *and* CHIPS *peep out, turning eyes up, holding out hats, some coins fall in the hats.* GIANT *pours money back into bags, putting them down with a thump.* EGG *and* CHIPS *disappear.*)

Put this safely away and bring me the hen that lays the golden eggs.

JILL. Yes, master.

(JILL *goes to chest, replaces money bags and brings hen to the* GIANT, *up at the table.*)

GIANT (*caressing hen*). Most precious of all my treasures. (*Makes passes into the air over the hen.*)

O, Bird beyond all price, lay me one of your golden eggs.

(*A golden egg is forthcoming.*)

Ha !—ha ! (*He holds up the egg, inspects it.*) Glorious! . . . Magnificent ! Jewel of jewels ! Bah ! I grow tired of my treasures too easily to-day. This strange odour makes me restless. There is a foreigner about. (*Cloth trembles again.*) I will walk outside and discover him.

(EGG *and* CHIPS *peep out under the cloth.*)

(*Exit* GIANT *up L.C.*)

(*Hen is left on the table.* EGG *and* CHIPS *make signs to each other about going, when* ODOR. *peeps out of cupboard and sees hen. Greed is shown on her face* (*licks her lips, etc.*) *She ventures out a few paces but a noise off sends her scurrying back. On tiptoe she comes to the table again, and picks up the hen, which starts to cackle loudly.* EGG *and* CHIPS *disappear.* ODOR. *makes for exit L. and trips. The* GIANT *rushes on and seizes her.*)

(*Pushing her downstage.*) Ah, so this is the strange smell. (*He examines her.*) What a curious bird. (*Pokes her with finger.*) Not much meat on it. Looks a bit sour too. You said there was no one here.

(ODOROUS *shivers and gurgles and moans with fear.*)

JILL. I—I didn't know there was. She must have got in whilst I was outside.

GIANT. Bah ! I could smell her a mile away.

JILL. But, master, I can't smell so well as you can.

GIANT. (*Roaring.*) *Anyone* could smell her ! (*To* ODOR.) What's your name ? Where d'you live ?

ODOR. (*trembling*). Odorous Egg, sir. By the Gas Works, sir.

(GIANT *roars with laughter.*)

GIANT. Well . . . (*He drags* ODOROUS *off R., leaving hen on table*) . . . I'll see what two weeks of Glaxo will make of you.

(*The others discreetly watch the* GIANT *exit.*)

JILL (*urgently*). Come out ! Come out !

(EGG, CHIPS *and* JACK *emerge from their hiding places.*)

He'll be away for a few minutes—it's your only chance !

EGG. Oh, I'll never leave mother again ! (*Bus.*)

CHIPS. I'll be a good boy after this ! (*Bus.*)

JACK. You cowards ! What about Odorous ?

JILL. He won't eat her yet, until she's fat !

CHIPS. Then she's safe for life !

EGG. I have an appointment !

(EGG *and* CHIPS *to door up L.C.*)

JACK. Jill darling ! (*Moves to her*)

JILL. Oh hurry ! All of you—hurry !

JACK. But aren't you coming with us ?

JILL. I daren't. I can't run very fast and he would catch us all if I came with you. No . . . you go . . . quickly.

JACK. I'm not going without you !

CHIPS. Come on ! Come on ! Or we'll all be sunk !

EGG. Jack ! I promised your mother to bring you home !

JACK. Jill, darling, you must come !

JILL. But if I do come I have no home or friends to go to.

JACK. We are all your friends.

CHIPS *and* EGG. Yes, we are, we are !

CHIPS. As long as we live !

EGG. But it won't be very long if we don't go !

JACK. Oh yes it will ! (*To* JILL.) And as for a home . . . why . . . wouldn't you share mine with me ?

JILL. Oh, yes ! I'd love to be your servant.

JACK. Servant ? Servant ? No ! My wife !

JILL. Your wife. Oh ! How lovely . . . oh, Jack, darling. (*They embrace.*)

EGG. My goodness ! Proposing ! In the jaws of death !

CHIPS. Eh ! Come on ! Break away !

(*They part.*)

If we don't get going . . . we'll be gone !

JACK. Come !

(*Exit* JACK, JILL *and* CHIPS *up L.C.*)

(*Egg goes to chest and gets money bags and takes hen from table.*)

EGG. Ee ! I've not been bailiff forty years for nowt !

(*Exit* EGG *carrying bags and hen which starts cackling.*)

(*Enter* GIANT *running. He sees hen has gone, rushes to the chest and finds money has also gone.*)

GIANT. They've stolen my hen ! They've stolen my gold ! (*Roars with rage.*) Thieves ! Robbers ! I'll have you alive or have you dead ! And grind your bones to make my bread . . .

(*Exit* GIANT, *roaring up L.C.*)

(CHIPS *throws open the window L., and jumps on the table, dashes across towards R. as* ODOROUS *rushes in R. They collide C.,* ODOROUS *screaming.*)

ODOR. (*clasping him*). Chippy ! Save me !

CHIPS. Save you ? What d'you think I came back for ?

ODOROUS. Chippy ! I'll marry you ! (*Kneels at his feet.*)

CHIPS (*declaiming*)

You may be scraggy—you may be lean,
You've an awful temper, and I know you're mean,
But oh ! Boy !
You're me old age pension !

(*Pulls her into his arms—B.O.*)

CURTAIN.

(*During Scene change : In front of tabs* CHORUS *enter (school children) as in Act I., or in speciality costumes) and go into a number, with refrain and dance*) . . .

No. 11. *Song.—Refrain and Dance......*

(CHORUS *of schoolchildren or villagers, etc.*)

ACT II. SCENE 3.

SCENE.—*The Road from the Castle.*

(*Same setting as Scene* 1.)

(*Curtain rises on dim blue lighting. Pink spots fade in on* FAIRIES *entering through cuts and P.S. entrance. Short dance, ending R., then retreating with beckoning steps, drawing on* JACK *and* JILL *from R. to C.* JACK *and* JILL *are apparently unaware of the* FAIRIES' *presence. They come C., weary and breathless and sink down C., the* FAIRIES *pointing to where they are to sit.*)

(*Exeunt* FAIRIES.)

(*Lighting comes up.*)

JILL (*breathless*). Oh . . . I can't go any further, Jack. My legs will scarcely move.

JACK. Courage, my darling, we haven't far to go.

JILL. I must rest awhile.

(FAIRIES *all point to the ground, C.* JACK *and* JILL *sit.*)
(*Exeunt* FAIRIES.)

JACK. Just a few minutes and then for the beanstalk, home and happiness.

No. 12. *Duet* ... ... JACK *and* JILL.

Are you ready now, sweetheart ? (*After number.*) (*Rises.*)

JILL (*rising*). Yes, Jack.

(*He puts his arm around her.*)

JACK. Then let us go. (*Points to opening down L.*) Look ! That must be the way !

(*Exit* JACK *and* JILL *into opening L.*)

(*Enter* EGG *R., running and panting. He pauses.*)

EGG. My legs . . . oh . . . my poor legs and bellicose veins. I've never run so fast and far since the day Barney's bull chased me. (*Confidentially.*) I'd been bathing and I'd only got my suspenders on, *joo know* . . .

(GIANT *is heard approaching.*)

. . . oooh ! . . . oooh ! He's coming !

(EGG *exits hurriedly L., to effect noise off.*)
(*Enter* GIANT, *R.*)

GIANT. Give me back my money-bags. Give me back my golden hen. I'll have your blood !

(*Exit* GIANT *L., to effect noise off.*)

(*Enter* ODOR *and* CHIPS, *R.* CHIPS, *carrying hen, is almost dragging* ODOR. *who is on the point of collapse.*)

ODOR (*gasping.*) I am undone. I am done up.

(*She collapses and* CHIPS *props her up.*)

CHIPS. 'Old on, old girl, 'old on. Here (*Gets bottle from pocket*) have a drink . . . this'll buck you up a bit.

(*She takes bottle and is about to drink when suspicion is shown.*)

ODOR. What's this—vinegar ?

CHIPS. No, you're all right this time. Drink up.

(*Cue for* CHIPS' *song*—" Oh, little hen " *or similar suitable number.*)

No. 13. *Song* ... ... CHIPS.

(ODOR *drinks, she likes it and drinks again. Drunken song* " Oh little hen "—*or other refrain.*)

CHIPS. 'Ere—go easy. You can't drink it like that.

ODOR. (*Giggles.*) I can . . . it's very nice . . . what is it ?

CHIPS. Aunty's ruin.

ODOR. I thought it was . . . (*Hiccup.*) T.N.T. (*Giggles.*) T.N.T. . . . charge it up to me.

CHIPS. Come on, now. We've got to catch up with Jack and the others.

(*He helps her struggle to her feet. She is slightly drunk*).

ODOR. Jack! I never want to see him again! You came back to rescue me! You are my hero! I promised you . . .

(*She clasps him to her.* CHIPS *struggles but can't get away.*)

I shall marry *you*! (CHIPS *faints.*) Ah, poor fellow. (*Hiccup.*) The sweet tidings were too much for him. I will revive him! (*Places bottle to raised head.*)

CHIPS. (*Moans.*) Save me! Save me!

(*Noises off.*)

What's that—the Giant!

(*Noise of* GIANT *off.* ODOR *screams.* CHIPS *scrambles up and both run off R.* GIANT *enters L.*)

GIANT. Ah! The old stinker . . . she has escaped! I missed her. Thud and blunder . . . Blood and thunder . . .

(*Exit* GIANT *R.*)

(*Lights fade quickly to roll of thunder, lightning flashes. Then flicker wheel on back cloth casts shadows of houses, and so on moving L., to R., as* EGG, ODOR, CHIPS *and—later—*GIANT *enter R., towards L., in the above order. By marking time, and moving forward slowly (each "running" step taking them forward very slightly) the effect of a realistic "chase" is secured. On exit L., they may run very quickly round behind cloth, re-appear R., and repeat the chase business. This should be done to suitable music, business, shouting and screaming and so on. When the stage is empty fade flicker wheel and bring in pink spots on* FAIRIES, *who enter. They draw* JACK *and* JILL *out from opening L., to up C. The Centre Cut is opened revealing stone steps, or a mound, backed by white sky backing, flooded gold and blue.*)

JACK. There it is, Jill! The beanstalk! Our journey is almost over. Come, let me help you.

(*Helps her up the steps. Tableau.*)

Look ! The garden !

(*They descend,* FAIRIES *close the cut. Enter* EGG, ODOR *and* CHIPS *at speed.*)

CHIPS. Where's that blinking beanstalk ?

(*Darting about the stage. They do not see the* FAIRIES.)

ODOR. Where ? Where? (*Darting about.*)

CHIPS. That's what I said. Think of something original. (*Collides with* EGG.)

EGG. Look !—up there ?

(*Fairies throw open the cut, now flooded pink. They dash for the cut and get there together.*)

CHIPS. One at a time. One at a time !

ODOR. Ladies first !

(*She pushes others aside and ascends.* GIANT *is heard approaching. They scream. Bus. of descending.*)

EGG. Quick ! Quick ! I hope we're at the bottom before the Giant comes. It won't bear all our weight. A-a-ah !

(*Roll of thunder. Quick fade to B.O.* FAIRIES *close the cut. Roll of thunder. Lighting fades in quickly. Enter* GIANT, *R.*)

GIANT. (*He darts here and there, drawn by the* FAIRIES *beckoning.*) Where are they ? Where have they gone ? Ah ! They think to escape. But I shall have them. The chase nears the end.

(*During the above the* FAIRIES *dance round him in a ring. He turns round and round in the reverse direction. Colour flicker wheel for effect. The* GIANT *very giddy.* FAIRIES *draw him up to C. cut and open it. It is now flooded green.*)

(*The* GIANT *ascends the mound (or steps). He roars. B.O., thunder, blue flash, showing* GIANT *throwing up his arms and collapsing. B.O., to more thunder and screaming wind as—*

THE CURTAIN FALLS.

(*During scene change: In front of tabs—Fairy dance or speciality number.*)

No. 14. *Dance,* or *Speciality Number.* THE FAIRIES

ACT II. SCENE 4.

SCENE —*The Cottage Garden*

(WIDOW *enters with broom and sweeps. She sighs heavily.*)

WIDOW. Oh dear. It's terrible dull without Jack here. He was a bad lad but he always livened things up. And now there's no one to cheer me. They've all gone. Even the Bailiff . . . he wasn't such a bad old egg either . . . I could have got on with him very nicely. Ah well . . . it's my own fault that they've gone. And that beanstalk's to blame. If that hadn't been there they'd still be here. Curse the thing. I'll see it gives no more trouble. I'll chop the dratted thing down.

(*Crosses stage and gets axe. Goes to beanstalk and and starts chopping clumsily.*)

This is the end of you. You (*Chop*) . . vile . . . (*Chop*) . . . vegetable. (*Chop.*) There's one for me (*Chop*) one for Jack (*Chop*) and one . . .

(*A shout is heard and she stops chopping and looks about.*)

JACK (*shouting*). Hey ! Oy ! Stop it ! Stop that chopping !

WIDOW (*drops axe—with joy*). It's Jack ! It's Jack ! Where are you, my darling boy ?

JACK Coming down !

(*Descends,* JILL *following. As* JACK *reaches the bottom,* WIDOW TWANKEY *goes to embrace him.*)

Just a minute, mother, there's someone else coming.

(JILL *reaches the bottom.* JACK *helps her.*)

Safe at last, my dearest. (*Brings her down R.C.*)

WIDOW (*following down L.C., staring*). Who is she ? What's her name ?

JACK. I know what it's going to be. Mother ! My future wife !

WIDOW. (WIDOW *reacts.*) But don't you know anything about her ?

JACK. I only know that her name is Jill (*puts his arm around her*). That we love each other and that I rescued her from Giant Snufflegobbler.

WIDOW (*amazed*). Jill! Giant Snooflegobler! Never 'eard of 'im! (*Cautious.*) How do you know her name is Jill?

JILL. I have a brooch with my name on. See! (*Shows* WIDOW *the brooch.*)

WIDOW (*looking at the brooch*). "Jill," and a crown! Why you . . . (*she drops a curtsey*) . . . Jack, you can't marry her.

JACK *and* JILL } Why not?

WIDOW (*slowly*). Well—er—you are—you haven't any money and you know I haven't.

(*The money-bags drop on the stage with a heavy thud.*)

EGG (*descending hurriedly*). Nay! There's money enough for them to marry on and to spare!

WIDOW. Mr. Egg! Oh Mr. Egg!

(EGG *comes down R. of* WIDOW TWANKEY.)

JACK. Egg! Where are the others?

EGG. Coming down . . . at least I passed something on the way that might have been them . . .

(*Noises off. He looks up.*)

Yes . . . here they come . . . and Chips has got another wedding present for you.

(ODOR. *and* CHIPS *descend—falling the last few feet. Uproar. Hen cackles, etc. Then the noise of* GIANT *descending as* ODOROUS *and* CHIPS *come down C., below the garden seat.*)

JACK. It's the Giant. He's coming down here.

WIDOW. What shall we do?

(*Retreating L. All re-group.*)

ODOR. Chips! Run for the Fire Brigade!

CHIPS. Run? What, again?

(GIANT *roaring off stage.*)

EGG. } Get the Fire Brigade! Get the Gas Department! (*Or local gags.*)

ODOR. } Get the Boys' Brigade! Get the District Council.

CHIPS. Where are they ?

WIDOW. Down at the "Bear." (*Or local hotel*).

(GIANT *roars.*)

CHIPS. Too late ! They don't close till two.

(*All look up, shouting* ad lib.)

JILL. What *shall* we do ? He's coming !

JACK. The axe, mother ! Where did you put the axe ?

(*They find the axe . . . sounds of* GIANT *nearer. The beanstalk is chopped away, and crashes off stage. The* GIANT'S *hat, stick, etc., may be dropped on the stage or a " dummy " of the* GIANT. JACK *rushes off through gate and above the wall. The women have covered their faces in horror at crash.*)

JACK (*returning*). It's all over. Giant Snuffle-gobbler is dead. Don't be frightened. Our worries are over. . . . Mother darling !

(*They embrace.*)

Jill sweetheart.

(*They embrace.*)

Mother,—Jill.

(*They embrace.*)

ODOR. (*snivelling*). Isn't it touching ? I want to cry.

(*Puts head on* CHIPS' *shoulder. He also starts to snivel.*)

I am enjoying myself !

CHIPS. I do love a good cry !

WIDOW. Oh, I'm so happy. (*Blubbers on* EGG'S *shoulder.*)

EGG. (*He joins in. Blubbering.*) Isn't it lovely ?

JACK (*laughing*). This happiness is all too much for me ! Come, Jill. (*Taking her up C.*) I am off to see the Parish Clerk, for this, my darling, is our wedding day !

(*They exit through the gate, and off S.L.*)

(WIDOW, ODOROUS, EGG, *and* CHIPS *go into number.*)

No. 15. *Song, Refrain and Dance*.......
...WIDOW, ODOROUS, EGG, CHIPS.

(*At conclusion of dance,* Odorous *and* Chips *are down R., and the* Widow *and* Egg *down L., as a fanfare of trumpets is heard off stage.*

(*A* Herald *and* Two Pages *enter up L. The* Herald *stands at the gateway, the* Pages *either side, below the gate.*)

Herald (*declaiming*). Her Royal Highness, the Princess Jill of Moldavia !

(*Fanfare off stage.*)

(*Enter* Jill, *in her Princess's dress, with* Jack, *gorgeously attired, on her left.* Odorous *and* Chips, Widow *and* Egg *move a little towards R.C., and L.C. bowing curtseying very low. Some villagers, children, etc., may enter down R. and L. and above wall, if available.*)

Jill. No, no, dear friends. I want no curtseys from you. But give us your good wishes for our happiness—it is all we ask.

Jack. Yes, mother, give us your blessing. The King has already done so.

Others. The King ?

Jack. Yes, for Jill is the King's daughter. She was stolen by the Giant when she was tiny.

Jill. And when we went to the Parish Clerk, he saw my brooch, which he remembered at my christening.

Jack (*excitedly*). He took us straight to the King !

Jill (*breaking in*). And when Jack found I was a Princess he said he couldn't possibly marry me.

Widow (*aside*). I knew it——

Jack. But she insisted ! She said she wouldn't be a Princess unless I married her.

Chips. Eh ! And what did King say ?

Jill. He made him a Prince at once ! He said he had always wanted a son.

(*All cheer. Bus. of excitement.*)

Jack. So we want you all to come to the wedding !

(*All crowd round* Jack *and* Jill, *shaking hands and kissing, etc.*)

(*During above bus.:—*)

Egg. Oh, thank you—I love a wedding !

Odor. How lovely—best wishes !

Widow. Oh, isn't it beautiful—I shan't go to the wukkus !

Chips. Ee—what a do ! And I'm marrying too ! (*Puts his arm round* Odor.'s *waist.*)

All. Why ?

Chips. Well——

All. BECAUSE SHE LIKES ME !

(*A happy moo-ing is heard off P.S. They all turn. Enter* Claribelle *led by* Old Woman, *L. They come down C.*)

All (*except* Jill). Claribelle !

(Claribelle *moos.*)

Jack (*embracing cow*). This is the one thing I wanted to complete my happiness.

Widow (*embracing cow*). My own sweet Claribelle ! And how well you look—and so plump !

(Claribelle *is bashful and makes a sign she wants to speak to* Widow *who bends an ear, and* Claribelle *moos confidentially.*)

Widow. No ! Are you really ? How nice for you . . . when ? . . . Oh, about April ? . . . Yes, of course I'll be there.

(Claribelle *registers content, as:*)

Jack (*to* Old Lady). Thank you a hundred times for being so good to Claribelle. I'd like to buy her back from you ? I'll give you any money—I'm ever so rich now.

(Claribelle *sits on her back legs L.C.*)

Old Lady. No ! You gave her to me when I was poor and lonely. And now I give back, in happiness to you. Now that you have your heart's desire, my work is done.

(Old Lady *drops her cloak, revealing herself as a fairy.*)

All. A fairy !

(*The* Fairy *stands on the garden seat.* Jack *and* Jill *kneel R. and L. of her as she raises her wand.*)

FAIRY My blessing on you all (*Waves her wand*) . . I give to you for all your days. Learn not to despise small, humble gifts. Take—and give—gladly. Help the poor, the sick, the lonely to smile through clouds and sunshine too. So may you learn to love and cherish one another and live—HAPPY EVER AFTER !

(*All into FINALE NUMBER.*)

No. 16. *Finale* ... ... FULL COMPANY.

CURTAIN.

ALTERNATIVE ENDING—

ALL. A Fairy !

(*The* FAIRY *stands on the garden seat.* JACK *and* JILL *kneel R. and L. of her.*)

Check lighting. Spot on FAIRY.

FAIRY (*raising her wand*).

My blessing, now the tale is told,
For all your days,—I now bestow.
May happiness be yours to hold
And bitter sorrow never know.

Omit if desired {
Do not despise the little gift
Although it be a bag of beans
Always the poor and fallen lift
Who've never known what pleasure means
}

Banish for ever hate and strife
Cherish each other, everyone.
So may you learn the joy of life
Leading the way towards—the SUN !

(*Lighting full up.*)

(*All come down and group for FINALE.*)

No. 16. *Finale* ... ... FULL COMPANY.

CURTAIN.

FURNITURE AND PROPERTY PLOT.

ACT I.

SCENE 1.

Garden seat. (C.)

Well, with rope and winding handle, bucket. (L.C.)

Garden broom.

Stool. (R.C.)

Basket of clothes. (*For* WIDOW.) Blue writ. (*For* EGG.)

SCENE 2.

Tree trunk. (R.C.)

Coins. (*For* JACK.)

Bag of beans. (*For* OLD WOMAN.)

SCENE 3.

Bag of beans. (*For* JACK.) Trick beanstalk (*up C., to grow* 3 *or* 4 *feet.*)

Stick. (*On stage, R.C., for* WIDOW.)

SCENE 4.

Beanstalk (*with hidden steps*)—set during B.O. after Scene 3.

Act II.

Scene 1.

Nil.

Scene 2.

Large kitchen table C., chair above, stools R. and L. of it.

Oak chest (at R.) containing:

Bag of gold coins.

Property hen, with golden eggs.

Cupboard (large enough to hide one person besides props.) containing:

Cake, jug of milk, plate, mug. (Jill.)

Bottle of vinegar.

Bag of potatoes.

Bag of flour.

Salmon tin (blue label).

Cookery book.

Large white table-cloth (to hang well down all round).

Scene 3.

Nil.

Scene 4.

Axe on stage. (R., by the stool.)

LIGHTING.

The Lighting Plot is designed for a fairly simple installation. It pre-supposes the existence of floats and sufficient battens for the depth of stage, and the provision of some spot lighting either from the " perches " or the front of house—the former is preferable. If possible, the cloths should be flooded from back stage in addition to, and sometimes instead of, the batten lighting. There is an electrical enthusiast attached to most amateur companies, so that usually a simple " dimmer " is obtainable. If not, the various colour circuits should be, if possible, on separate switches so that something like a " fade-in " and " fade-out " is secured even if not so effectively ar with a dimming apparatus. The colour and flickes wheels can always be hired from any stage electrical firm. The colour numbers indicated are those of the Strand Electric Company, and are, generally speaking, universal.

Needless to say, pantomime depends greatly on lighting for some of its most attractive effects, so that any extra trouble and expense in this department will yield a generous dividend in the popularity of the show.

The producer who can boast of a spot batten will, of course, adapt the lighting plot for their employment.

The electrician will have to provide " flash boxes" (always within the limits of statutory regulations) and synchronise these with the thunder and wind effects.

Where no perches are possible, one or two floods or spots from the front of the house may be employed. They may also be combined with perches if the latter are installed.

LIGHTING PLOT.

ACT I.

SCENE 1.

Floats and battens, amber, pink, white, full.
Flood cloth straw.
Amber lengths on cottage interior backing.
Perches spot PRINCIPALS for Numbers, Surprise Pink and White, as desired.
No cues.

SCENE 2.

Floats and battens, amber, pink, white—full.
Flood straw on cloth.
No cues.

SCENE 3.

Floats and battens, amber, pink, blue $\frac{3}{4}$.
Flood cloth No. 4 amber, and No. 10 pink.
Interior lengths amber.
Perches No. 52 gold, frost, on C. acting area.

Cue:

As ODOROUS exits shaking her fist:—

Fade-out all lighting, as JACK settles to sleep, to nil except blues at $\frac{1}{4}$. Then bring in colour wheel on FAIRIES for Ballet (No. 6), fading the same out on their exit, and blues to nil. During Ballet, a blue spot on "beanstalk" as it grows.

During the B.O., music continues. Tabs may be drawn to set grown beanstalk.

Fade-in on:—

SCENE 4.

To open: Slow fade-in of floats and battens (except batt. lighting cloth), blue only to $\frac{3}{4}$, then pinks to $\frac{1}{4}$, and bring both to $\frac{1}{2}$, as flood on cloth pink and blue on P.S. section only. No light from flood or batt. on O.P. section.

As opening scene proceeds: Bring all lighting in as in Scene 1, except white in floats and batts; Flood cloth No. 19 or 20 blue, P.S. section only. No batt. light on cloth.

Act II.

Scene 1.

To open : Fade-in blue of floats and battens, and flood on cloth, to $\frac{1}{4}$. If no spots, battens pink $\frac{1}{2}$.

Entrance of Fairies: Spot from perches or battens No. 7 pink and No. 16 blue. Pink frost spot on Jack.

Exeunt Fairies: Fade out spots Bring up blues and pink in floats and batts to $\frac{1}{2}$. Spot Jack as before. Spot Old Woman No. 16 blue.

Exit Old Woman: Spot Fairies on entrance as before, and Jack, to exit.

Entrance of Odor., Egg, Chips: Perches flood C. area.

End of scene: B.O.—green flash—B.O.

After Sc. 1 (*front of tabs.*). Floats and No. 1 Batten full up. Perches spot Widow white and pink.

Scene 2.

Floats and battens, amber, pink—full. White $\frac{3}{4}$.

Amber lengths on interior backings.

Flood cloth straw and pink.

Spot Principals for Numbers, No. 7 pink and white frost.

Cue: Chips: " You're me old age pension." (*Bus.*) *B.O.*

After Scene. (*Front of tabs.*). Floats and battens full up.

Perches if needed.

Scene 3.

To open: Floats, battens blue $\frac{1}{4}$, and flood on cloth, No. 17, blue frost. Spot Fairies pink, as before, and follow. P.S. perch No. 7 pink on Jack and Jill as they enter R.

Cue 1. *Exeunt* Fairies: Fade out spots on Fairies. Pink and blue spots mingle on Jack and Jill (from perches). At the same time bring up floats and battens blue, pink, amber to $\frac{1}{2}$.

Cue 2.—*After Duet* (*No.* 12): White spot on opening in wing down L., faded as JACK and JILL exit.

Cue 3.—*2nd exit of* GIANT: Check all except blues to nil, including flood on cloth. Blue ¼. Flash of lightning. Thunder. Then bring in the flicker wheel to cast moving shadows of houses, etc., for " run across " and bus. After bus. Flicker off.

Cue 4.—*Re-enter* FAIRIES. Spot as before. (These spots come in as flicker fades out.)

Cue 5.—*Re-enter* JACK *and* JILL: Pink spot follows up to C. as FAIRIES open cut in cloth. (For this: Flood sky-cloth behind cut No. 52 and No. 16.)

Cue 6.—*Cloth Cut bus. for* ODOR., EGG, CHIPS: As before, with flood on cloth behind No. 11 pink. Thunder—B.O.

Cue .7—*Enter* GIANT: Change spots for dance and bus., to colour flicker wheel, then B.O. as FAIRIES open cut and reveal cloth behind flooded green. Then B.O., blue flash, thunder, and screaming wind as GIANT collapses.

After Scene: (*front of tabs.*) Floats, No. 1 Batt, and perches as required for Speciality Number.

SCENE 4.

As for ACT I, SC. 1. Perches spot Principals for Numbers and C, acting area, white frost and pink for the FINALE.

MADE AND PRINTED IN GREAT BRITAIN BY
BUTLER & TANNER LTD, FROME AND LONDON
MADE IN ENGLAND